101
QUESTIONS & ANSWERS
How Things Work

WHO? WHAT? WHERE? WHY?

WHERE? WHY? WHO? WHAT? HOW?

WHO? WHAT?

WHO? WHAT? WHEN? HOW? WHERE? WHY?

WHO? WHAT? WHEN? HOW? WHERE? WHY? WHO?

HAMLYN

GLOSSARY

aerial A metal rod or a dish used to change electrical signals into radio waves at a transmitter or radio waves into electrical signals at a receiver.

atom Tiny particle of matter, too small to be seen even with a microscope. Each atom contains a clump of particles (protons and neutrons) at its centre, the nucleus, surrounded by particles called electrons.

battery A device that changes chemical energy into electricity.

camshaft A spinning rod with projections (cams) on it that push the valves open inside an engine.

catalyst A substance that speeds up a chemical reaction without being used up itself.

compressor A turbine used to squeeze more fuel and air into an engine than it could normally suck in.

crankshaft The main rod, or shaft, inside an engine. The spinning crankshaft is linked to the wheels and makes them spin too.

diaphragm A thin sheet of material, usually metal, used in telephones. Its vibrations help turn sound into electrical signals at the mouthpiece and electrical signals into sound at the earpiece.

digital watch A watch that shows the time as numbers (12.43 for example) instead of a pair of hands on a dial.

distillation The process of making a liquid purer by heating it so that it evaporates and then cooling it so that it turns back into a liquid.

evaporate Change from a liquid to a vapour (gas). When water is boiled, it evaporates and turns into steam.

fuel A material like coal, wood, gas or oil that is burned to release energy stored inside it.

gears Interlocking toothed wheels that reduce the high speed of an engine to the lower speed of the vehicle's wheels.

infra-red Invisible radiation that is just beyond the red end of the rainbow colours of visible light.

laser A device that produces a very intense beam of light.

lens A piece of glass or clear plastic shaped so that it bends light. Depending on the shape of the lens, it may make things look bigger or smaller than they really are.

liquid crystal display (LCD) A screen used in digital watches, small television sets, pocket calculators, some video games and other electronic equipment. An electrical signal from the equipment makes a special liquid trapped inside the screen change and part of the screen darkens. By turning different parts of the screen on and off, an LCD can make letters, numbers and pictures.

microprocessor A computer's master control chip. It contains the Central Processing Unit (CPU) which directs all activities inside the computer.

molecule A clump of atoms, anything from two atoms to thousands of atoms.

radio A system for sending and receiving information over long distances in the form of invisible waves of energy.

tonne A measure of weight, equal to 1,000 kilograms.

turbine A rod, or shaft, with angled blades, driven by a flow of liquid or gas. The liquid or gas pushes against the blades and makes them spin.

valve A device that controls the flow of fuel and air inside an engine. One set of valves open to let fuel and air into the engine and, when the fuel has been burned, a second set of valves open to let the exhaust gases out.

x-rays Radiation that can pass through materials normally opaque to us.

First published in Great Britain in 1993 by
Hamlyn Children's Books
an imprint of Reed Children's Books
Michelin House, 81 Fulham Road
London SW3 6RB and Auckland, Melbourne, Singapore and Toronto.

Copyright © Reed International Books 1993

Designed and Produced by Lionheart Books, London

ISBN 0-600-58025 3

British Library Cataloguing-in-Publication Data. A catalogue record for this book is available from the British Library.

Printed in Italy

Acknowledgements
Designer: Ben White
Project Editor: Lionel Bender
Text Editor: Madeleine Samuel
Media Conversion and Typesetting: Peter MacDonald and Una Macnamara
Managing Editor: David Riley
Artwork: pages 4, 5, 6-7, 13b, 14, 16-17, 18, 23t, 24-25, 29, 30, 32, 33, 35b, 36, 37, 38, 39cr and b, 41b, 42b, 43, 45, 46-47 by The Maltings Partership; 8-9, 10, 15, 26, 31 by Ian Thompson/Art Beat; 11t Hamlyn Children's Books; 11b by Gerald Whitcomb; 12, 13, 27, 28 by Roger Courthold; 19t, 22-23, 40 by David Russell; 20, 21b, 42t, 44 by Colin Corbishley; 21t by Art Beat/Richard Dunn; 34, 35t, 38-39, 41c by Andrew McGuinness. (top = top, b = bottom, l = left, r = right, c = centre).

CONTENTS

This book contains questions and answers on the following topics:

ENERGY & POWER

Electricity	4
Nuclear Energy	6
Alternative Energy	8
Electric Motors	10
Engines	12

AT WORK

Computers	14
Photocopiers and Faxes	16
Lifts, Escalators, Air Conditioning	18
Medical Machines	20

INDUSTRY

Metal	22
Drilling for Oil	24
Petrochemical	26
Coal and Water	28
Paper and Printing	30

AT HOME

Household Appliances	32
Timekeepers and Calculators	34
Locks and Keys	36
Telephones	38

ENTERTAINMENT

Music, Records and Discs	40
Sound and Vision	42
Recording Equipment	44
Photography	46
Index	48

Ian Graham

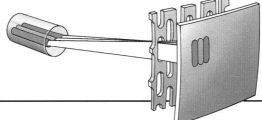

Where does electricity come from?

The electricity that lights our homes and powers our television sets, washing machines and other appliances is made in power stations. Inside them, a fuel such as coal, oil or gas is burned to heat water in a boiler and turn it into steam. The steam flows through propeller-like turbines and makes them spin. The turbines are linked to generators. These are coils of wire free to rotate between magnets. Magnetic forces acting on the spinning coils make electricity flow in the wire.

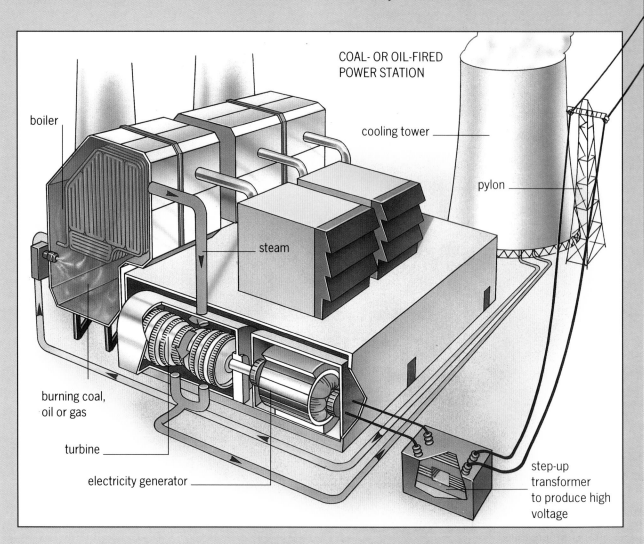

COAL- OR OIL-FIRED POWER STATION

boiler

cooling tower

pylon

steam

burning coal, oil or gas

turbine

electricity generator

step-up transformer to produce high voltage

WHAT IS CURRENT?
An electric current is a flow of electricity. When electricity flows, it can do work. It might light a bulb, or operate a computer game.

WHAT IS AN AMP?
The energy and speed of an electric current is measured in units called amperes, or amps. They are named after the French scientist Ampère.

WHAT IS A VOLT?
The strength of the force that makes an electric current flow is measured in volts. A typical torch battery has a voltage of 1.5 volts.

How does electricity reach homes?

At the power station, a device known as a step-up transformer boosts the electricity to a very high voltage, between 100,000 and 700,000 volts. The electricity travels to surrounding towns along cables hanging from towers called pylons.

Before it makes the final part of its journey into offices, factories and people's homes by underground cables, a series of step-down transformers reduce its voltage to the lower level used there (between 110 and 240 volts).

DID YOU KNOW...

● Power stations have to provide more electricity at certain times of the day? There may be a surge in the need for power during an interval in a television film, when millions of people make a hot drink at the same time!

● The round towers at power stations are cooling towers? Cold water from a nearby river cools the steam pipes from the turbines so that the steam changes back into water. This water is led back to the boiler. The river water becomes heated and some of it turns to steam, which escapes from the towers.

● When the electricity supply to an area is cut off, perhaps due to a fault, the absence of power is called a black-out because all the lights go out?

● When the power supply falls in voltage but is not cut off completely, this is called a brown-out?

● The world's worst power-cut, in the USA and Canada in 1965, blacked out 30 million people's homes?

● The electric current generated by power stations is called AC, or alternating current, because it reverses direction continually (see motors on page 10).

WHAT IS THE GRID?

The network of cables and transformers that connects power stations to all the homes and businesses using electricity is called the national grid.

power station

electrified railway

heavy industry

light industry

farm

village

city

How is nuclear energy produced?

You and everything around you, including this book, are made from tiny particles of matter called atoms. At the centre of each atom is a clump of even tinier particles called the nucleus. An enormous amount of energy is locked up inside this microscopic speck of matter. It is known as nuclear energy. Nuclear power stations are designed to release this energy and use it to make electricity.

WHAT ARE FUEL RODS?

Nuclear power stations use a fuel called uranium. The uranium, which is mined from the ground, is packed into pipes known as fuel rods. Heat from nuclear reactions in the rods is collected by a liquid or gas circulating between them. The heat is used to turn water into steam. The steam turns a turbine linked to a generator which makes electricity.

HOW MUCH ENERGY?

Nuclear fuel is packed with much more energy than coal, oil or gas. One tonne of uranium can produce as much energy as 20,000 tonnes of coal.

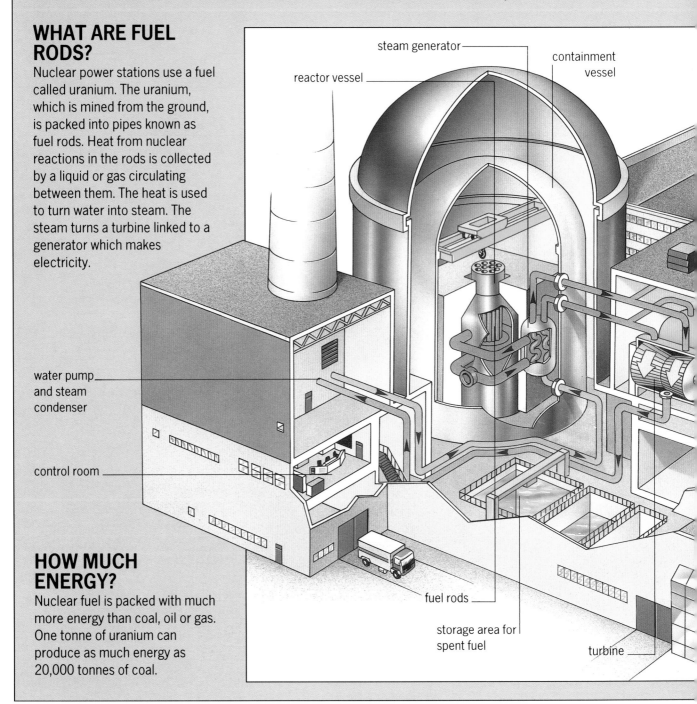

steam generator

reactor vessel

containment vessel

water pump and steam condenser

control room

fuel rods

storage area for spent fuel

turbine

WHY SPLIT ATOMS?

Uranium is not burned to release energy in the same way as coal. The uranium atom is the biggest in nature. It splits apart very easily and, as it does, it releases a burst of energy. This is called nuclear fission. It also spits out two particles, called neutrons, which can strike two more uranium atoms and split them. The continuing process is called a chain reaction.

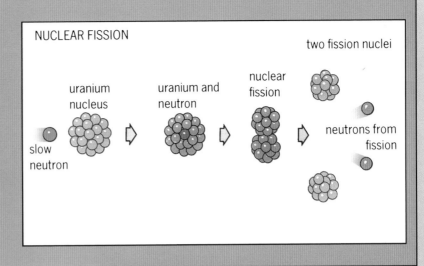

NUCLEAR FISSION

uranium nucleus

slow neutron

uranium and neutron

nuclear fission

two fission nuclei

neutrons from fission

NUCLEAR FISSION REACTOR AND POWER STATION

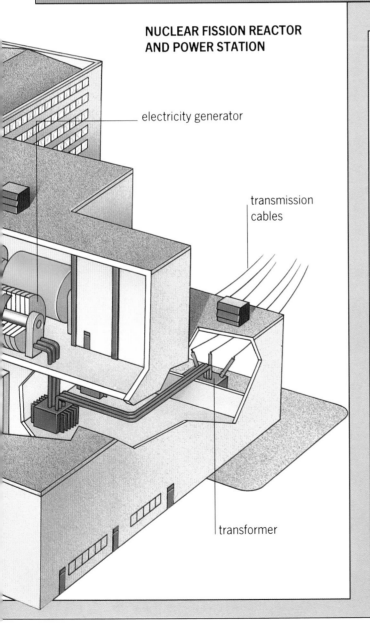

electricity generator

transmission cables

transformer

WHAT IS NUCLEAR FUSION?

● Future nuclear power stations may obtain energy by nuclear fusion not fission. This works by fusing (joining together) very small atoms.
● Nuclear fusion reactors use as a fuel the lightest element of all, hydrogen.
● Inside a fusion reactor, hydrogen gas is kept in place by strong magnets and is heated to the high temperature (millions of degrees) needed for fusion to take place.
● Stars shine because of energy released in their nuclear fusion.

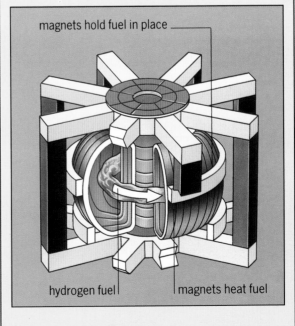

magnets hold fuel in place

hydrogen fuel

magnets heat fuel

What is the alternative?

The coal, oil and gas that we burn to make electricity now will run out one day and our other main source of electricity, nuclear power, is dangerous. Alternative energy from safe and continuing sources such as the Sun, wind and water will be needed to replace them.

Why are modern windmills thin?

Old windmills had to be large brick buildings because people worked inside them turning wheat into flour. Modern windmills are used in a completely different way. They turn wind into electricity. No-one works inside them, so the towers that hold them up can be much thinner.

How can water light up a city?

The modern waterwheel is the water turbine used in large dams. When water flows through the turbine's angled blades, the force of the water pushing against the blades makes the turbine spin. A generator linked to it also spins and produces electricity which is supplied to people's homes. Electricity made from water in this way is called hydroelectricity.

WHY ARE DAMS CURVED?
Dam walls are usually curved because this gives them great strength and enables them to resist the force of water pressing on them from the reservoir.

HOW MUCH POWER?
Water is the most widely used of all the natural sources of energy. More than a fifth of the world's electricity is already made from water in hydroelectric power plants.

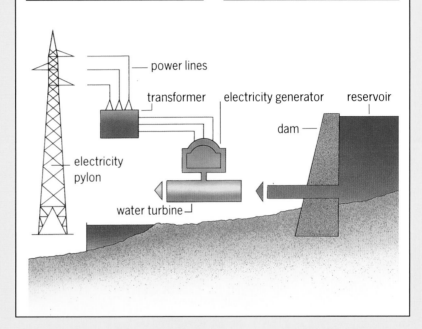

power lines

transformer   electricity generator   reservoir

dam

electricity pylon

water turbine

How can the Sun heat bath water?

HOW MUCH ENERGY?
Only 1/100th of the Sun's radiated energy reaches the Earth's surface. The rest is reflected into space and soaked up by the air.

Shallow trays called flat plate collectors on a building's roof heat water by the action of sunlight. They work like greenhouses, trapping heat under their glass tops. Water flowing through pipes in the collector absorbs this heat.

Why do electric motors turn?

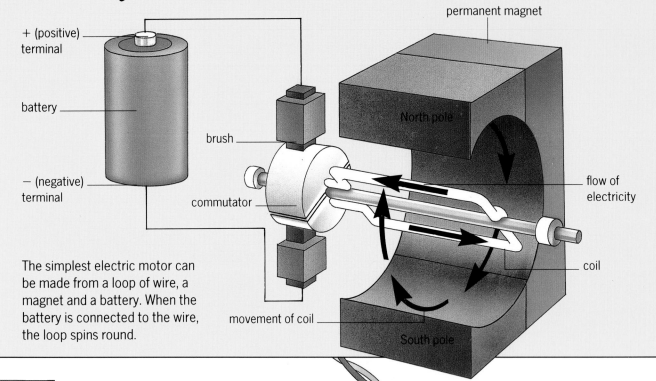

+ (positive) terminal

battery

− (negative) terminal

brush

commutator

permanent magnet

North pole

flow of electricity

coil

movement of coil

South pole

The simplest electric motor can be made from a loop of wire, a magnet and a battery. When the battery is connected to the wire, the loop spins round.

What is inside an electric motor?

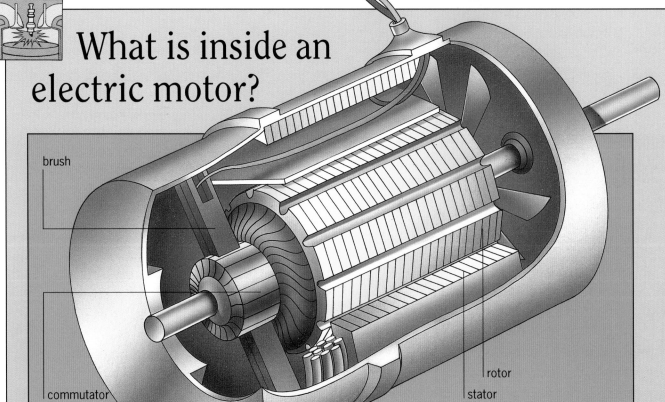

brush

commutator

rotor

stator

Motors work because magnets push against each other. One of the magnets is made from a coil of wire magnetised by passing an electric current through it. When this is placed inside a second magnet, they push against each other and the coil turns. The commutator, which consists of two half-circles of metal attached to the ends of the coil, reverses the battery connections to the coil every half-turn and keeps the motor turning.

HOW OLD ARE MOTORS?

In 1821, the great English scientist Michael Faraday built a machine to show how electricity and magnetism could produce movement. He had invented the electric motor.

A single coil of wire and a magnet make a very weak motor. More powerful motors use many coils of wire in the central turning part, the rotor. The commutator has many segments too, one for each coil. More coils wrapped around the rotor form the stationary part of the motor, the stator.

Why are some trains electric?

Many of the world's trains, including the 200kph French TGV, are powered by electric motors, because they are cleaner and more efficient than engines that burn petrol or diesel oil.

DID YOU KNOW...

In many big cities, electric trains carry passengers through tunnels under the ground? They can travel right across a busy city quickly because they avoid traffic jams on the surface. The first underground railway was opened in London in 1863. There are also major underground rail systems in Paris, New York and Moscow.

ELECTRIC TRAINS

TGV

How do engines make things move?

Engines work by burning a fuel to release the energy stored inside it and using the energy to move wheels, propellers or turbines. Coal and wood are unsuitable fuels for modern vehicles because they give out energy too slowly when they burn. Petrol and oil are the most popular, because they burn more easily and give out energy very quickly.

DID YOU KNOW...

● Petrol is ignited inside an engine by an electric spark from a spark plug in each cylinder?
● The burning fuel and air expand and push a piston down a cylinder?
● Most cars, buses and trucks have four or eight cylinders?
● The pistons turn the crankshaft, which is linked to the wheels by a set of gears which vary the speed of the road wheels?
● The first practical petrol engine, the forerunner of the modern car engine, was made in 1885 by Karl Benz in Germany?
● The 'cc' of a car engine stands for cubic centimetre. It is a measure of the volume of air the pistons push aside in the cylinders.

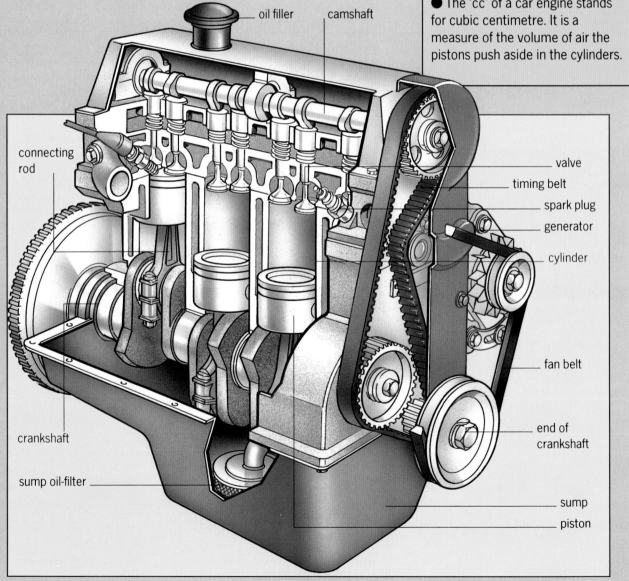

oil filler

camshaft

connecting rod

valve

timing belt

spark plug

generator

cylinder

fan belt

end of crankshaft

crankshaft

sump oil-filter

sump

piston

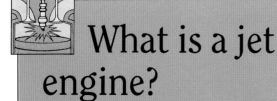

What is a jet engine?

Jet engines, or gas turbines to give them their correct name, propel most of the world's airliners and combat aircraft. Air is sucked in at the front of the engine by a spinning fan. Inside the engine, it is squeezed by a spinning compressor turbine and forced into a combustion chamber. There, fuel is sprayed into the air and burned. The hot gases expand and rush out of a pipe at the back of the engine.

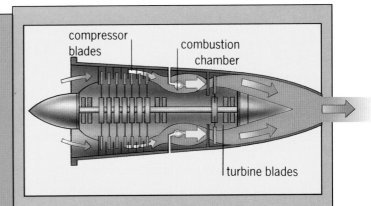

compressor blades

combustion chamber

turbine blades

WHAT IS A TURBOJET?

The simplest and earliest type of jet engine is the turbojet. This narrow powerful engine is used by the fastest aircraft. The supersonic airliner Concorde is powered by four Olympus turbojets.

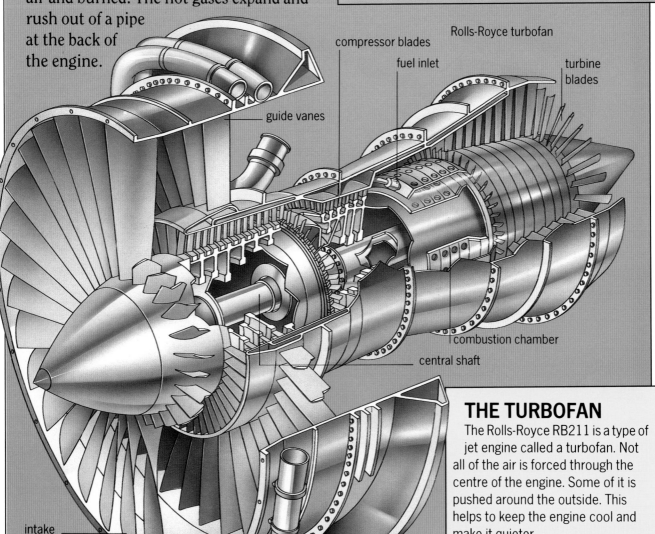

Rolls-Royce turbofan

compressor blades

fuel inlet

turbine blades

guide vanes

combustion chamber

central shaft

intake fan

THE TURBOFAN

The Rolls-Royce RB211 is a type of jet engine called a turbofan. Not all of the air is forced through the centre of the engine. Some of it is pushed around the outside. This helps to keep the engine cool and make it quieter.

How do computers work?

A computer is a super-fast electronic calculator. Information entered via the keyboard is changed into numbers and stored in the computer's memory or on a magnetic disc called a floppy disc. The microprocessor processes the information and shows the results on the screen.

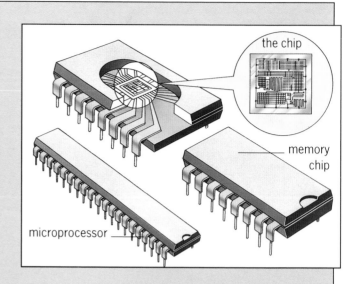

the chip

memory chip

microprocessor

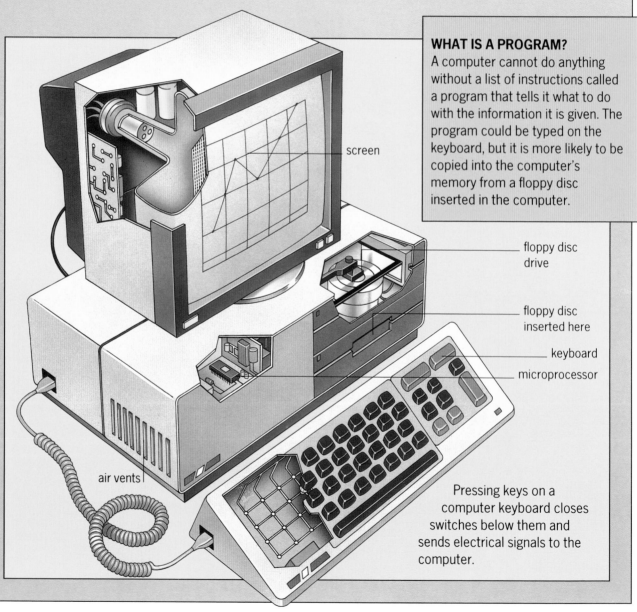

screen

WHAT IS A PROGRAM?
A computer cannot do anything without a list of instructions called a program that tells it what to do with the information it is given. The program could be typed on the keyboard, but it is more likely to be copied into the computer's memory from a floppy disc inserted in the computer.

floppy disc drive

floppy disc inserted here

keyboard

microprocessor

air vents

Pressing keys on a computer keyboard closes switches below them and sends electrical signals to the computer.

14

How do shops use computers and lasers to save work?

At a supermarket check-out, a laser "reads" a code on each item and passes it on to the shop's computer. The computer knows which item the code refers to and sends the correct price to the till. The laser check-out saves work because people no longer have to enter each price individually. Information about sales can also be analysed by the computer more quickly than by a person.

photodetector

mirror

light source

lens

bar code

WHAT ARE BAR CODES?

A bar code is a series of parallel black lines. As a light is moved across it, the beam is reflected more by the white spaces between the lines than by the black lines. The reader detects these reflections and changes them into an electrical signal that a computer can process. This bar code is being scanned by a reader shaped like a pen.

HOW DO LASERS READ?

Underneath the check-out, a laser beam is bounced off spinning mirrors to make it sweep to and fro across anything held above it. Reflections of the bar code, are picked up by a photodetector.

bar code on item

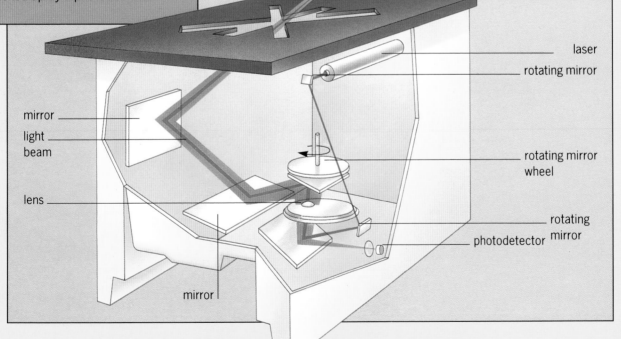

mirror

light beam

lens

mirror

laser

rotating mirror

rotating mirror wheel

rotating mirror

photodetector

How do photo-copiers work?

Modern photocopiers use a process called xerography, a word formed from two Greek words meaning dry writing. An image of what you want to copy is reflected onto an electrically charged drum coated with a material like selenium, so that the charge leaks away where light falls on it. Toner, a fine black powder, sticks to the charged areas. When this is transferred onto a sheet of paper, the result is a photocopy.

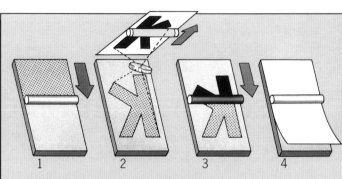

1 2 3 4

HOW DOES IT COPY?

The metal plate or drum is electrically charged (1). The image is reflected onto the plate (2). A dusting of toner sticks to the image (3). Paper is pressed onto the plate (4). The paper picks up the image (5) and is heated to make a permanent copy (6).

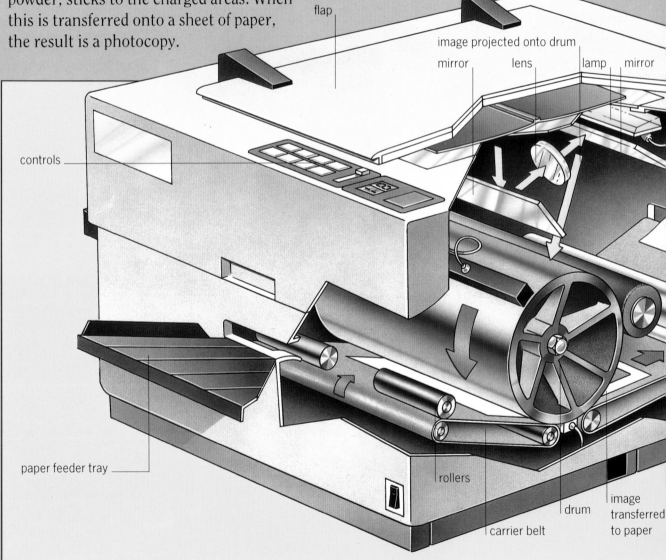

flap

image projected onto drum

mirror   lens   lamp   mirror

controls

paper feeder tray

rollers

drum

image transferred to paper

carrier belt

5   6

How are printed papers and pictures sent by telephone?

Printed words and pictures can be sent along ordinary telephone lines by facsimile, or fax, machines. One machine converts printed matter into electrical signals and sends it by telephone to another fax machine. This converts the signals back into print.

When a sheet of printed paper is fed into a fax machine, motorised rollers pull the paper inside the machine and an intense light illuminates it. The printing is reflected onto a light sensitive cell line by line. This converts it into electrical signals which are sent down the telephone line.

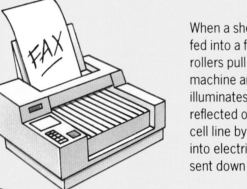

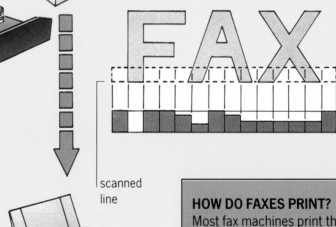

scanned line

tray for finished copies

heated rollers

Modern photocopiers are compact automatic machines. Some can make copies in different sizes. Others can make colour copies.

HOW DO FAXES PRINT?
Most fax machines print the messages they receive on thermal paper, a special type of paper that turns black when heated by an electric current passing through it. Thermal paper is more expensive than ordinary paper. The latest "plain paper" fax machines use a dry powder process that can print on ordinary paper.

How do lifts carry people to the top of skyscrapers?

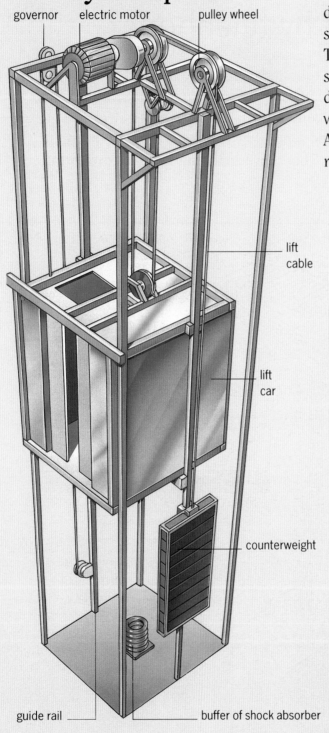

governor · electric motor · pulley wheel

lift cable

lift car

counterweight

guide rail · buffer of shock absorber

Lifts are essential for travelling up and down tall buildings quickly. A lift car is suspended by a cable attached to its roof. The cable runs up to the top of the lift shaft, over a pulley (a grooved wheel) and down again to a weight that balances the weight of the lift car and its passengers. A powerful motor turns the pulley to raise or lower the car.

DID YOU KNOW...
● The tallest building in the world, the Sears Tower in Chicago, USA, has 103 lifts to carry people up and down its 110 floors?
● Lifts have built-in safety devices to ensure that they cannot fall down the shaft? The first lift we know about was built specially for King Louis 15th of France in 1743?
● The first lift used by the public was built by Elisha Graves Otis in New York and opened on March 23rd 1857?

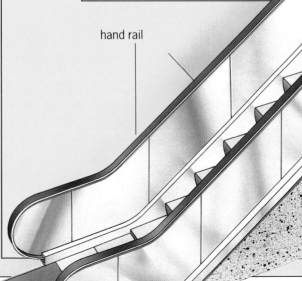

hand rail

Why have air conditioning?

Air inside a skyscraper would soon become stale and smelly if it were not constantly filtered and mixed with fresh air from outside. This is done by the air conditioning system, which also heats or cools the air.

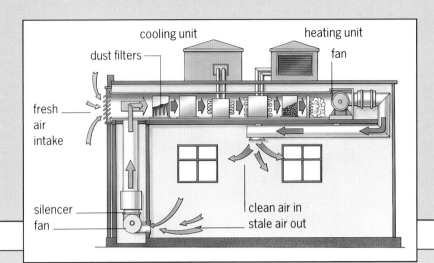

How does an escalator work?

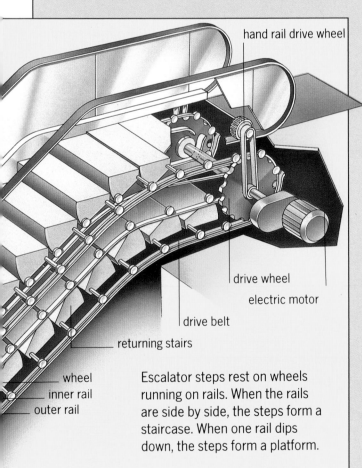

The most efficient way of moving people from one floor to the next inside a building is by an escalator, a moving stairway. Its steps are linked together in an endless loop and driven by an electric motor. At the top and bottom, the steps are lowered to form a flat platform to make it easier to get on and off. The handrail also moves in time with the steps so that the passengers can hold on.

Escalator steps rest on wheels running on rails. When the rails are side by side, the steps form a staircase. When one rail dips down, the steps form a platform.

DID YOU KNOW...
● The escalator was invented in 1892 by two Americans, Jesse W Reno and George H Wheeler?
● It was not called an escalator until Charles D Seeberger thought of the name in 1899?
● The first escalator for public use was opened in 1900 at the Universal Exhibition in Paris? When the exhibition closed, it was moved to Gimbel's Department Store in Philadelphia, USA.
● The world's tallest building, the Sears Tower, has 18 escalators?

What if your kidneys fail?

Our kidneys filter waste chemicals out of our blood. If they stop working, a kidney machine is used instead to clean the blood. The patient is linked to the machine two or three times a week by two tubes. One takes blood from the body and the other returns it after it has passed through the artificial kidney.

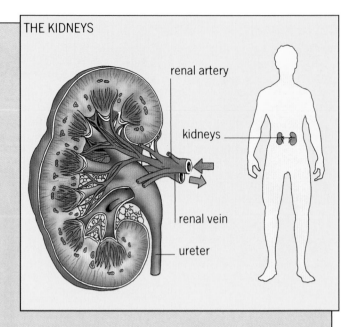

THE KIDNEYS

renal artery

kidneys

renal vein

ureter

The kidney machine (left) does the same job as our much smaller natural kidneys (above). The process of cleaning the blood by means of a kidney machine is called dialysis.

KIDNEY MACHINE

pressure gauge

bubble catch

artificial kidney pump and heater

from artery

to vein

tank for dialysis liquid (salt solution)

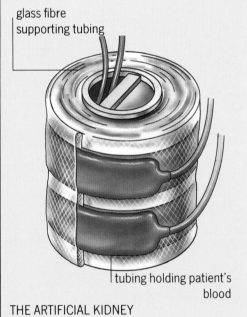

glass fibre supporting tubing

tubing holding patient's blood

THE ARTIFICIAL KIDNEY

The patient's blood flows through a tube lying in a salty liquid. Water and chemicals pass through the tube into the salt solution.

How can we see unborn babies?

A probe resting on a pregnant woman's abdomen (tummy) sends out bursts of sound so high in pitch that they cannot be heard. This "ultrasound" bounces harmlessly off the baby. The reflections, or echoes, bouncing back are picked up by a detector inside the probe and a moving picture made of the baby.

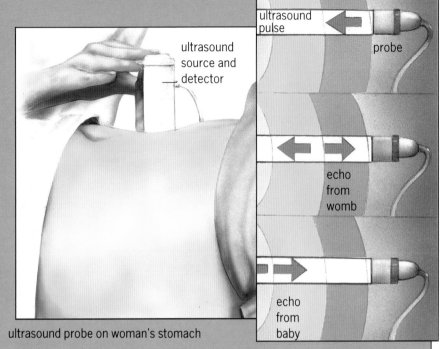

ultrasound probe on woman's stomach

womb — abdomen
ultrasound pulse
probe
echo from womb
echo from baby
ultrasound source and detector

How does a body scanner work?

An X-ray machine rotates around the patient firing X-rays through the body from different angles to detectors on the other side. A computer converts the information from the detectors into a picture of a slice through the body. The motorised couch moves forward a fraction and the process is repeated to make a picture of another slice.

WHAT IS TOMOGRAPHY?
This type of body scanner is also called a computerised tomography (CT) scanner. The word tomography comes from the Greek word tome, which means slice.

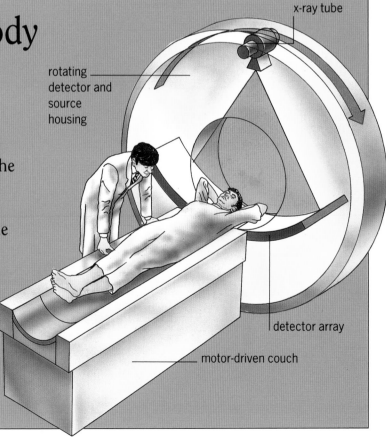

x-ray tube
rotating detector and source housing
detector array
motor-driven couch

How is iron made into steel?

Steel is a very useful material for making things because it can be pressed and bent into almost any shape. It is made from iron and iron is made from iron ore. The iron ore, coke (made by heating coal) and limestone are loaded into the top of a blast furnace, a tall cylinder 50 metres high and 15 metres across. Hot air is blown in through holes called tuyres around the bottom. The coke burns, melting the iron ore and producing molten pig iron, an impure form of iron. The pig iron is converted to steel by removing most of the carbon. This is done in a converter. Some limestone (to remove impurities) and scrap steel may be added too. Oxygen is blown through the mixture to remove the carbon, leaving molten steel. This is poured into moulds, where it solidifies.

WHAT IS STEEL?

Steel is an alloy (a mixture) of iron and carbon. Pig iron contains too much carbon, making it brittle. When most of this is burned out in a steel converter, the product is an alloy of iron with only a few parts per thousand of carbon. This small amount of carbon makes steel stronger and harder than pure iron.

Scrap steel, limestone and molten iron are loaded into the steel converter. Oxygen is blasted in through a pipe and molten steel is poured out.

HOW FAST IS IT?

Steelmaking is a very fast process. Once the furnace is loaded and oxygen is blasted in through a lance (a pipe), 300 tonnes of pig iron can be converted to steel in only half an hour.

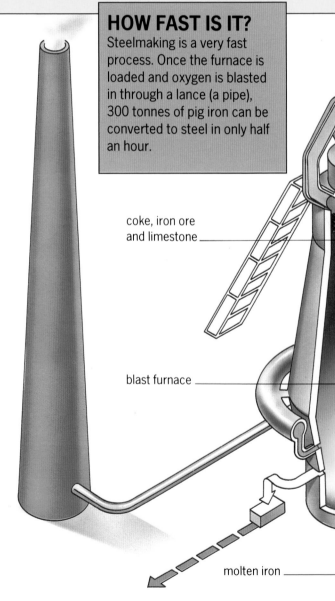

coke, iron ore and limestone

blast furnace

molten iron

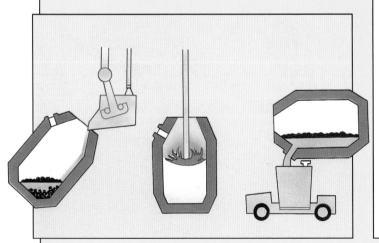

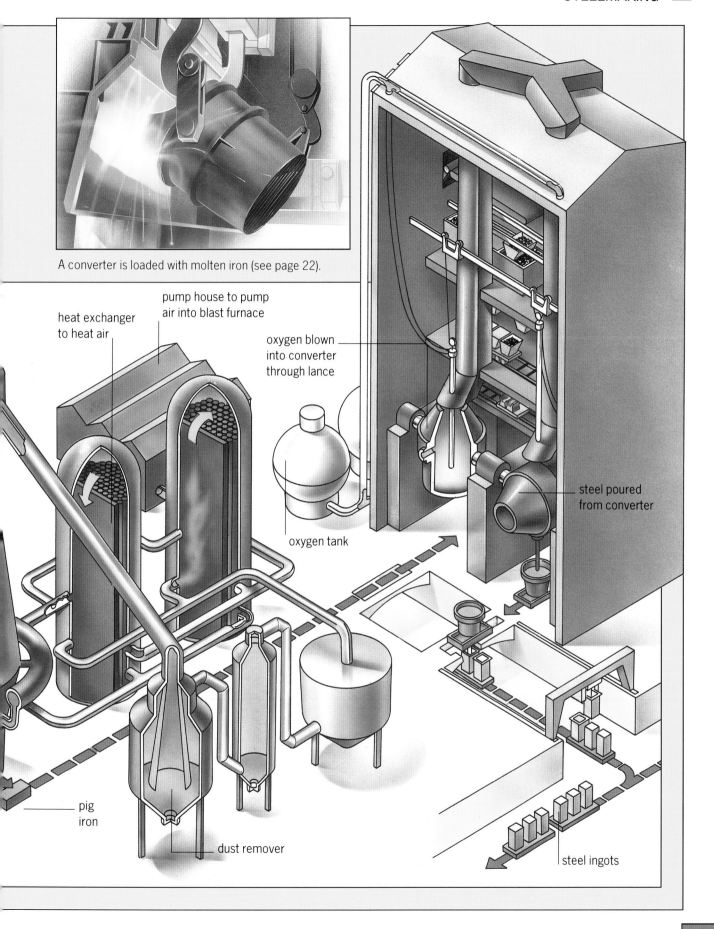

A converter is loaded with molten iron (see page 22).

heat exchanger
to heat air

pump house to pump
air into blast furnace

oxygen blown
into converter
through lance

oxygen tank

steel poured
from converter

pig
iron

dust remover

steel ingots

Where does oil come from?

Millions of years ago, the bodies of microscopic organisms that had lived in the sea sank to the seabed and became covered with layers of sand and fine sediment. This covering kept oxygen out and stopped the organisms from rotting away altogether. Instead, bacteria changed them into oil (or into natural gas). As more sediment piled up on top, its weight pressed the underlying layers into rock and trapped the oil beneath them. It stayed there until people learned how to extract it by drilling through the rock. Pockets of natural gas are usually found above oil fields.

There are different types of drilling rigs for reaching oil under the sea. Some float (left), anchored to the seabed. Others stand on steel legs (centre). Production platforms (right) have tanks where oil is kept until it can be taken ashore.

DID YOU KNOW...

● The Chinese were probably the first people to drill for oil using bronze tubes and bamboo more than 2,000 years ago?

● The world's first modern oil well was drilled in 1859 at Titusville, Pennsylvania in the USA by Edwin L. Drake?

● Between 1939 and 1979, oil production increased tenfold, from 300 million tonnes per year to more than 3,000 million tonnes?

● The first offshore drilling rig was used to drill for oil off the coast of California in 1897?

● When existing reserves of fossil fuels like oil are used up, there will be no more?

● Every year we burn oil that took nature one million years to make?

● We will probably begin to run out of oil some time during the 21st century?

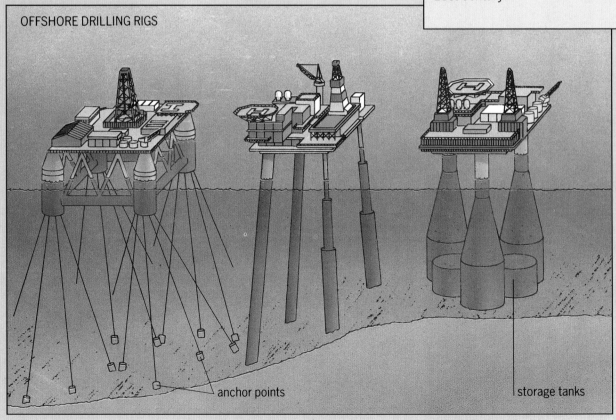

OFFSHORE DRILLING RIGS

anchor points

storage tanks

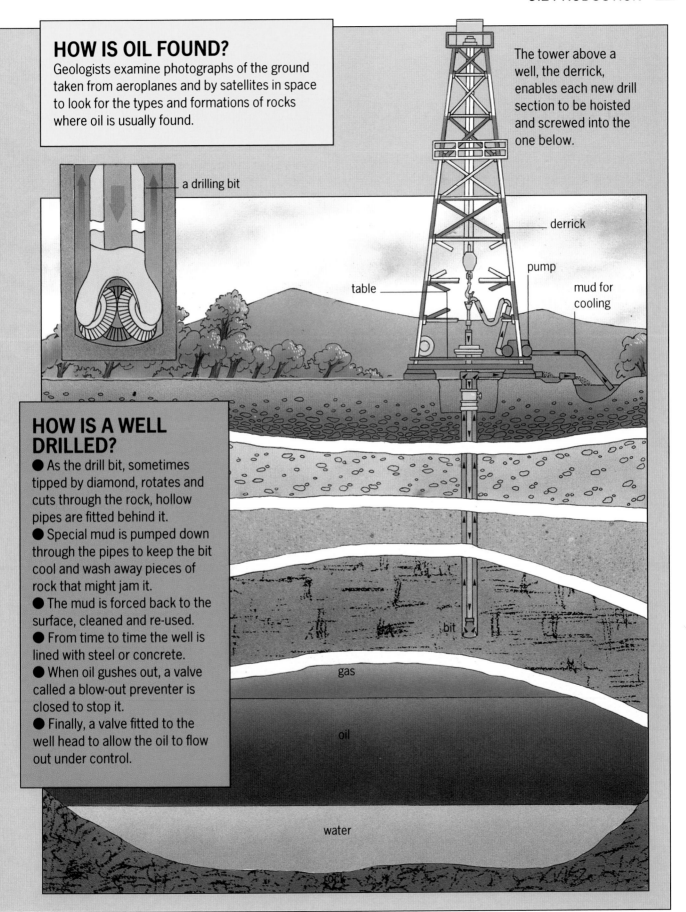

HOW IS OIL FOUND?
Geologists examine photographs of the ground taken from aeroplanes and by satellites in space to look for the types and formations of rocks where oil is usually found.

The tower above a well, the derrick, enables each new drill section to be hoisted and screwed into the one below.

a drilling bit

derrick

pump

table

mud for cooling

HOW IS A WELL DRILLED?
● As the drill bit, sometimes tipped by diamond, rotates and cuts through the rock, hollow pipes are fitted behind it.
● Special mud is pumped down through the pipes to keep the bit cool and wash away pieces of rock that might jam it.
● The mud is forced back to the surface, cleaned and re-used.
● From time to time the well is lined with steel or concrete.
● When oil gushes out, a valve called a blow-out preventer is closed to stop it.
● Finally, a valve fitted to the well head to allow the oil to flow out under control.

bit

gas

oil

water

rock

25

How is oil made into plastics?

Refining oil to make useful chemicals and other materials begins by heating it. The vapours it gives off are pumped into a distillation column. The thinnest vapours rise to the top, forming petrol and gas. Lower down, diesel fuels form. Waxes and bitumen sink to the bottom.

DID YOU KNOW...

● The distillation column, or fractionating tower, is the tallest part of an oil refinery, standing up to 80 metres high.
● The different parts of oil separated in a refinery are known as "fractions".
● Some fractions, petrol for example, can be used as they come off the column, but others need more processing to purify them.
● Oil is sometimes combined with a substance called a catalyst that "cracks" (breaks down) the heavier fractions of the oil?

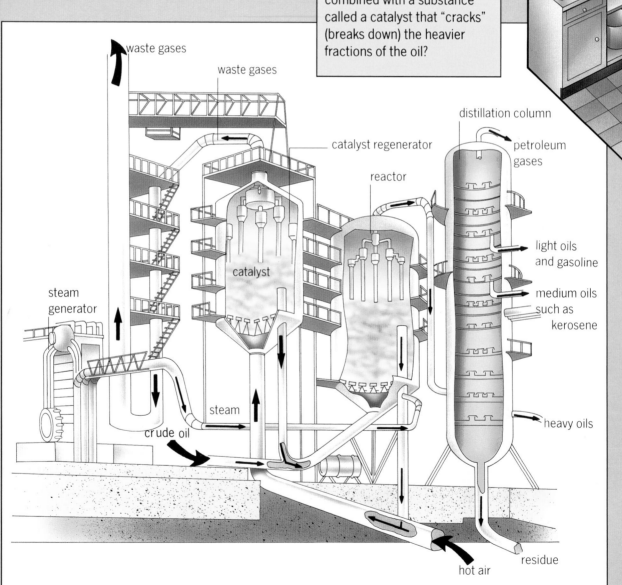

waste gases

waste gases

catalyst regenerator

reactor

distillation column

petroleum gases

catalyst

steam generator

light oils and gasoline

medium oils such as kerosene

steam

crude oil

heavy oils

hot air

residue

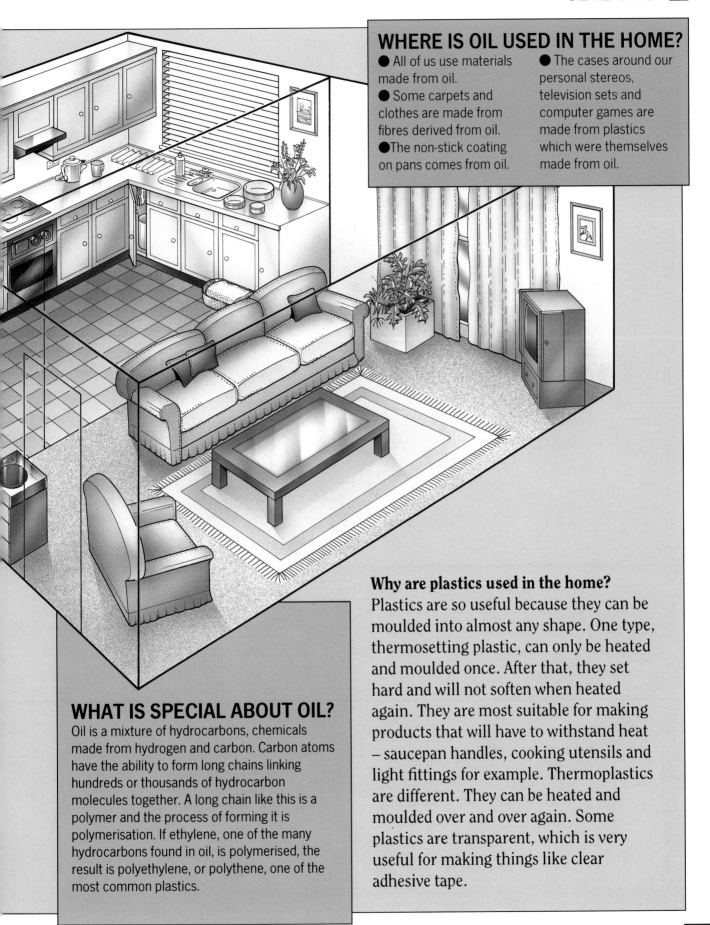

WHERE IS OIL USED IN THE HOME?

- All of us use materials made from oil.
- Some carpets and clothes are made from fibres derived from oil.
- The non-stick coating on pans comes from oil.
- The cases around our personal stereos, television sets and computer games are made from plastics which were themselves made from oil.

WHAT IS SPECIAL ABOUT OIL?

Oil is a mixture of hydrocarbons, chemicals made from hydrogen and carbon. Carbon atoms have the ability to form long chains linking hundreds or thousands of hydrocarbon molecules together. A long chain like this is a polymer and the process of forming it is polymerisation. If ethylene, one of the many hydrocarbons found in oil, is polymerised, the result is polyethylene, or polythene, one of the most common plastics.

Why are plastics used in the home?

Plastics are so useful because they can be moulded into almost any shape. One type, thermosetting plastic, can only be heated and moulded once. After that, they set hard and will not soften when heated again. They are most suitable for making products that will have to withstand heat – saucepan handles, cooking utensils and light fittings for example. Thermoplastics are different. They can be heated and moulded over and over again. Some plastics are transparent, which is very useful for making things like clear adhesive tape.

How is coal dug up?

Modern coal mines have at least two vertical shafts. One carries miners and their equipment underground. Coal is brought out through the other one. Fresh air is pumped down to the miners through one shaft and stale air escapes through the other. A network of horizontal tunnels is dug into the coal seam from the vertical shafts. Strong "props" stop the roof from falling in while machines in the tunnels grind

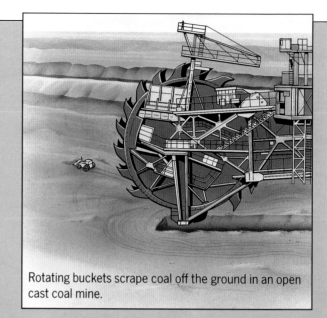

Rotating buckets scrape coal off the ground in an open cast coal mine.

away at the coal. It falls onto a conveyor belt which carries it back to a vertical shaft where it is lifted to the surface. The coal is stored in huge open mounds.

direction of air flow

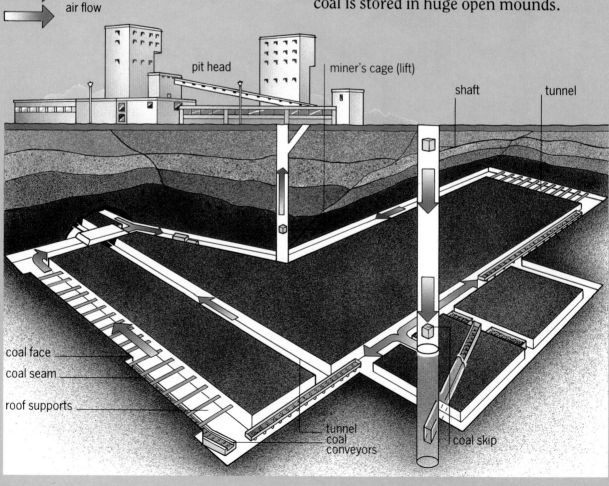

pit head

miner's cage (lift)

shaft

tunnel

coal face

coal seam

roof supports

tunnel coal conveyors

coal skip

Where does tap water come from?

The water most of us drink comes from reservoirs, or artificial lakes. Water treatment plants make it safe for us. Large particles sink to the bottom of sedimentation tanks or are trapped by pumping the water through sand. Chlorine is added to kill germs. The water is stored in huge tanks.

DID YOU KNOW...
● Almost three quarters of the Earth's surface is covered by water but only a tiny fraction of that (3 percent) is fresh water?
● More than three quarters of that tiny fraction of fresh water is frozen at the poles?
● And most of the rest is hidden deep underground?

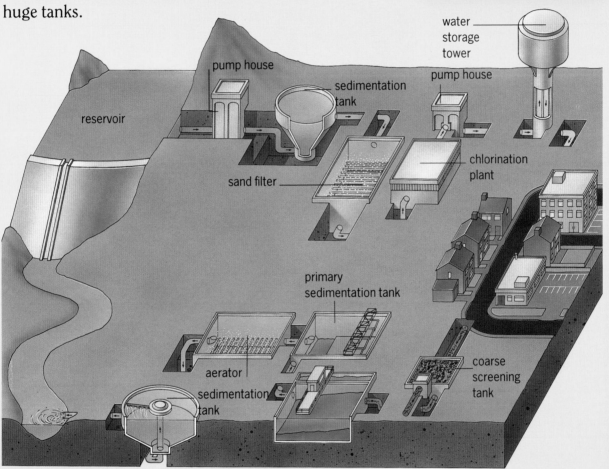

reservoir

pump house

sedimentation tank

sand filter

water storage tower

pump house

chlorination plant

primary sedimentation tank

aerator

sedimentation tank

coarse screening tank

WHY TREAT WATER?
In the days when water was not purified before people drank it, infected water supplies caused outbreaks of killer diseases like cholera. There are still many places in the world where tapwater is not safe to drink.

HOW MUCH DO WE USE?
In the past 50 years, the amount of water we use has trebled. Some of us use more than others. Americans use about 2,300 cubic metres each per year. Many people in developing countries each use less than 50 cubic metres.

WHERE DOES RAIN GO?
Most of the rain that falls on the land evaporates back into the sky again and most of the rest runs off the land into the sea. Dams and reservoirs help to trap some of the run-off so that we can use it.

How is pulp made into paper?

Papermaking begins with a porridge-like pulp of shredded wood. Chemicals in the pulp separate the wood fibres. The pulp is spread on a moving wire or plastic mesh belt. Some water drains through the mesh and suction extracts even more. The paper is moved onto a felt belt and pressed to take out more water. Heated rollers complete the drying process. Finally, the paper is fed through a series of polished rollers to smooth its surface and rolled onto a large reel.

HOW OLD IS PAPER?

The ancient Egyptians were making papyrus, a sort of paper, from reeds 5,000 years ago, but it was the Chinese who first made fine writing paper in about AD100.

Paper is made by giant machines 100-200 metres long that can produce more than a kilometre of paper every minute.

HOW MUCH IS USED?

It takes approximately 12 trees to make one tonne of paper. Every year a forest the size of Sweden has to be cut down to provide the world with paper.

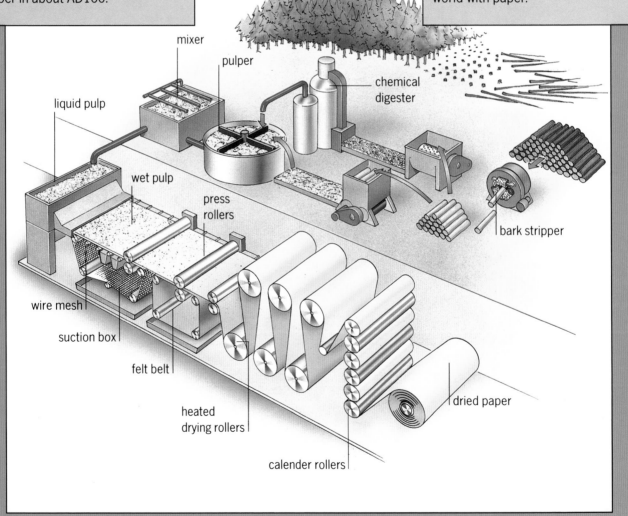

mixer
pulper
chemical digester
liquid pulp
wet pulp
bark stripper
press rollers
wire mesh
suction box
felt belt
heated drying rollers
dried paper
calender rollers

How are papers printed?

Early printing presses worked by pressing raised inked letters against the paper. This method, letterpress, is still used, but two other methods are more popular. Gravure uses a printing plate etched (eaten into) by acid. Ink fills the pits left by the acid. Lithography uses a printing plate treated so that the ink sticks to some parts of the smooth printing plate but not others. All three methods use curved printing plates wrapped around cylinders. Motors drive them at high speed, printing on a web (a very long continuous roll of paper).

DID YOU KNOW...
● The Chinese printed the first books more than 1,000 years ago?
● Printing came to Europe in about 1447 when the German printer Johannes Gutenberg designed a printing press with movable type, characters that could be rearranged to make any words?
● To print in colour, four plates print the cyan (blue), magenta (red), yellow and black parts of an image on the same piece of paper?
● Modern printing presses not only print, they also cut the paper, put the pages in the right order and fold them in the right place?

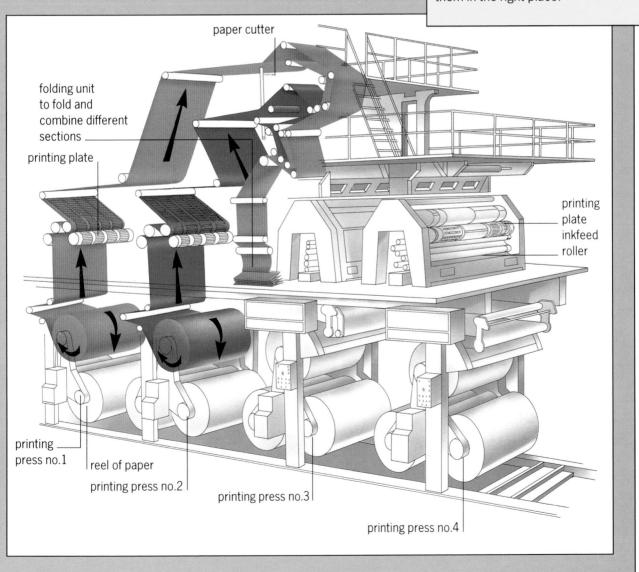

paper cutter

folding unit
to fold and
combine different
sections

printing plate

printing
plate
inkfeed
roller

printing
press no.1

reel of paper

printing press no.2

printing press no.3

printing press no.4

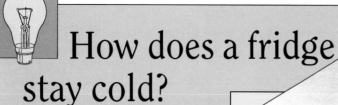

How does a fridge stay cold?

A gas, the refrigerant, is compressed by a motor until it forms a liquid. This flows through pipes inside the refrigerator, where it evaporates. The energy it needs to change into a gas is absorbed as heat from the refrigerator's contents which become cooler. The refrigerant is then compressed into a liquid and used again.

HOW DO YOU MAKE IT COLDER?
A refrigerator's temperature is set by a thermostat, a switch that turns the compressor on and off.

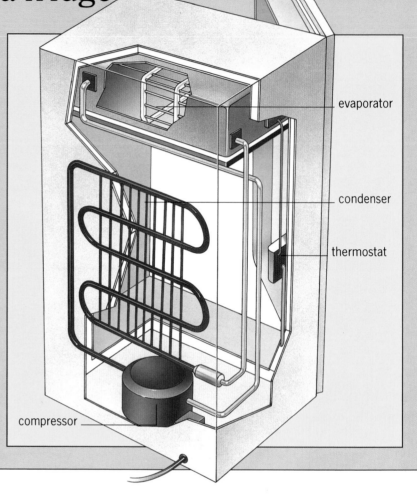

evaporator

condenser

thermostat

compressor

How do vacuum cleaners work?

An electric motor spins a fan which sucks air in at one end of the cleaner and blows it out at the other end. The flow of air is so strong that it lifts dust and dirt out of the carpet. A dust bag and filter inside the vacuum cleaner lets the air flow through but traps the dust and dirt.

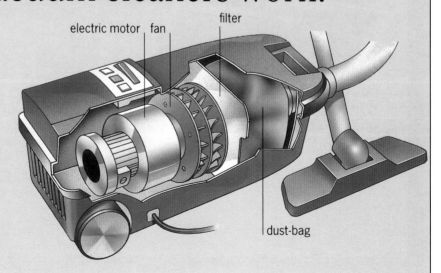

electric motor   fan   filter

dust-bag

What happens inside a washing machine?

Clothes in the tub are soaked and agitated in hot or cold water and washing powder according to programs stored in the control unit's memory. The length of wash is adjusted for the type of material of the clothes.

WHY IS WASHING SPUN?

At the end of a wash, a washing machine drum spins very quickly. The clothes are pushed against the drum, squeezing most of the water out. The water then drains away.

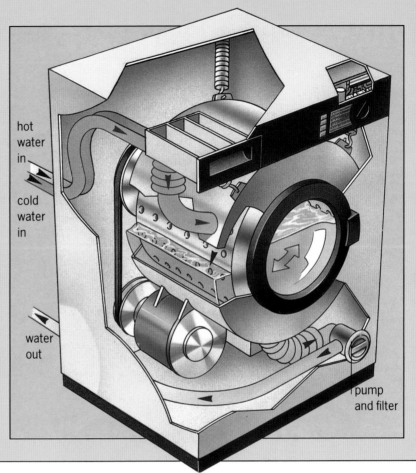

hot water in

cold water in

water out

pump and filter

How does an iron work?

An electric element inside the iron heats the sole plate. In a steam iron, water drips through holes in this plate and turns to steam. Moistening the material with steam helps the hot iron to flatten the creases.

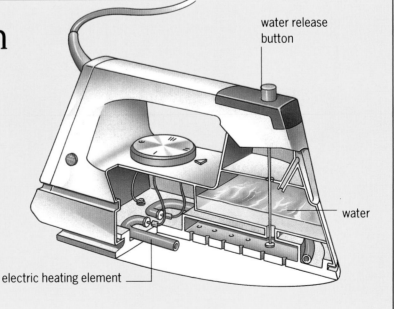

water release button

water

electric heating element

Why are there cogs and wheels inside clocks?

Clocks and watches have two main parts – the drive wheel and the escapement. The drive wheel moves the hands. The escapement ensures that the hands turn at the right speed to keep good time. The cogs and wheels link the escapement, drive wheel and hands together. The energy to keep the mechanism going is supplied by a coiled spring, a falling weight or a battery.

WHY DO CLOCKS TICK?

Tall clocks like grandfather clocks use a pendulum, a weight hanging on a rod, to keep good time. As it swings to and fro, it rocks an anchor. This lets the drive wheel rotate a little on each pendulum swing. It is the anchor catching the drive wheel that makes the ticking sound. When the drive wheel moves, a weight hanging from it falls a little and gives the pendulum a kick to keep it swinging.

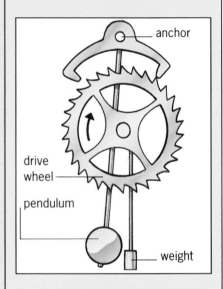

anchor

drive wheel

pendulum

weight

In smaller clocks and watches, a balance wheel driven by a tiny hairspring turns to and fro instead of a pendulum. A coiled mainspring keeps the mechanism going.

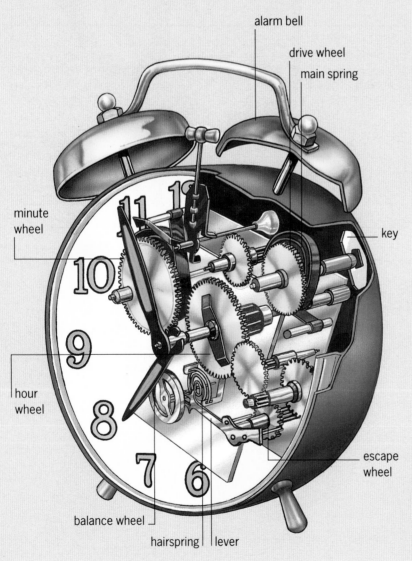

alarm bell

drive wheel

main spring

minute wheel

key

hour wheel

escape wheel

balance wheel

hairspring lever

THE BALANCE WHEEL CLOCK

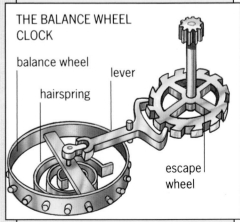

balance wheel

hairspring

lever

escape wheel

How can a crystal tell the time?

An electric battery replaces springs and falling weights as the energy source in a digital watch. A microchip counts the regular vibrations of a quartz crystal. The crystal's rapid vibrations are electronically divided down to provide the slower electrical pulses that operate the liquid crystal display where the time appears.

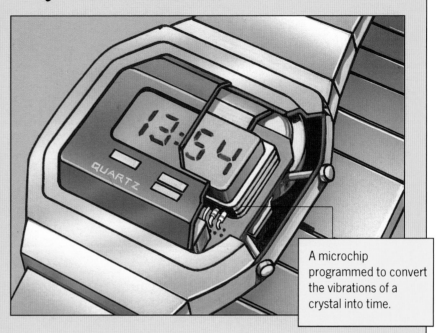

A microchip programmed to convert the vibrations of a crystal into time.

How does a calculator do sums?

Like a digital watch, an electronic calculator has a liquid crystal display (LCD) driven by one or more microchips. In the case of the calculator, however, the chips are programmed to add, subtract, multiply and divide numbers entered on the keyboard. The sequence of steps required to do a simple calculation is shown. The numbers on the display are made by turning on some or all of the display's segments.

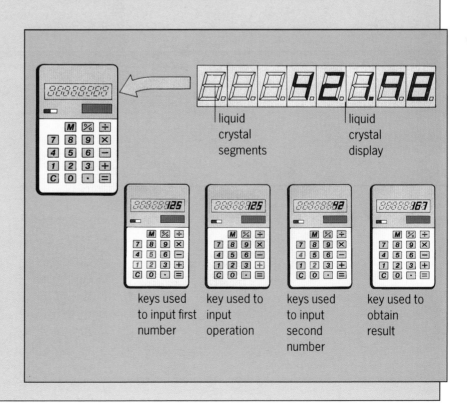

liquid crystal segments

liquid crystal display

keys used to input first number

key used to input operation

keys used to input second number

key used to obtain result

How do locks in my house work?

There are many different ways of sealing a door. You might tie it closed, stick it with adhesive or brick it up, but any door sealed like this would take a long time and lot of effort to open again. A lock allows a door to be sealed securely and opened again easily IF you have the right key. A bolt from the lock fits into a hole in the door frame and jams the door closed. Only the correct key will fit the lock and withdraw the bolt so that the door can be opened again.

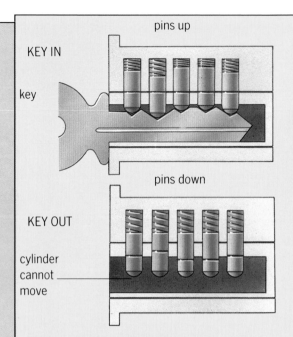

THE CYLINDER LOCK

When a key is inserted in a cylinder lock, it lifts pins inside the lock. Only the correct key will lift each pin by the right amount so that the cylinder can turn and open the lock.

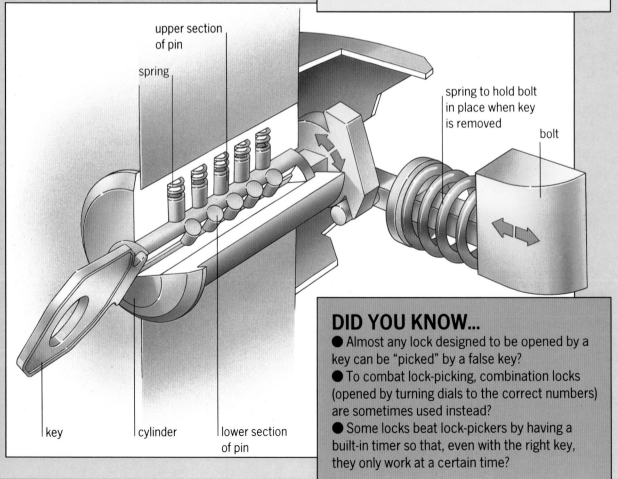

DID YOU KNOW...
● Almost any lock designed to be opened by a key can be "picked" by a false key?
● To combat lock-picking, combination locks (opened by turning dials to the correct numbers) are sometimes used instead?
● Some locks beat lock-pickers by having a built-in timer so that, even with the right key, they only work at a certain time?

Do all locks work in the same way?

The second major type of lock, the lever-tumbler lock, works in a different way from the cylinder lock. A spring holds a lever-tumbler against the bolt, which can only be slid out to lock the door, or in to open it again, if the correct key lifts the lever. Turning the key slides the lever and the bolt attached to it. For extra security, some of these locks have several levers. Each has to be raised to a different height to free the bolt and operate the lock.

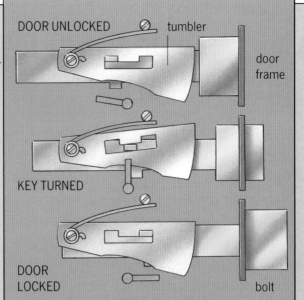

DOOR UNLOCKED — tumbler — door frame

KEY TURNED

DOOR LOCKED — bolt

LEVER-TUMBLER LOCK

A lever-tumbler mechanism is held open (top) by a bolt pin in a slot. The key lifts the lever and it slides forwards, pushing the bolt into the door frame (middle). The lever drops again, locking the bolt pin in the slot (bottom).

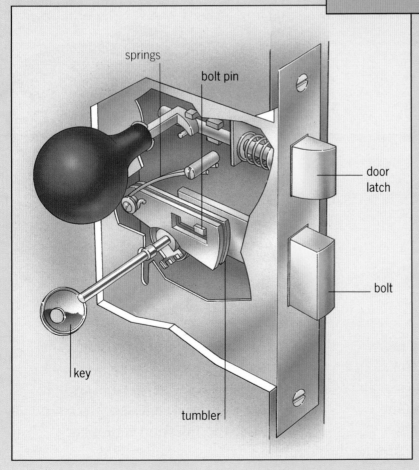

springs
bolt pin
door latch
bolt
key
tumbler

DID YOU KNOW...

● The cylinder lock often used on front doors today works in the same way as wooden locks used by Ancient Egyptians 4,000 years ago?

● The modern cylinder lock was invented in 1848 by an American, Linus Yale?

● Yale's design for the popular cylinder lock was inspired by locks found in the pyramids in Egypt?

● Modern electronic combination locks open only when the correct sequence of numbers is entered by means of a keypad on the door?

● Private information stored in computers is sometimes "locked" away so that it can only be called up onto the computer's screen by typing the right password, a secret word, on the keyboard?

How does a telephone work?

When you speak into a telephone, the vibrations in the air caused by your voice make a diaphragm vibrate. This squeezes grains of carbon under the diaphragm and changes their resistance to an electric current flowing through them. The current changes in step with your voice. It travels along the wire to the telephone you are speaking to at the other end of the line. The changing electric current varies the strength of a magnet which makes a diaphragm vibrate and makes the sound of your voice in the other telephone's earpiece.

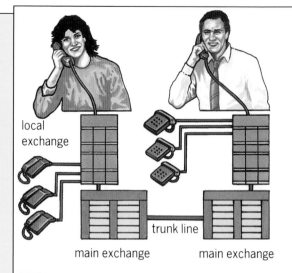

local exchange

trunk line

main exchange   main exchange

TELEPHONE EXCHANGE
Any two telephones can be linked together by switching them onto the same line through local and main telephone exchanges.

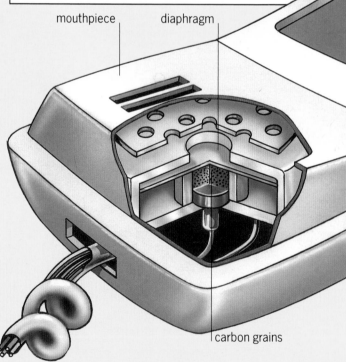

mouthpiece   diaphragm

carbon grains

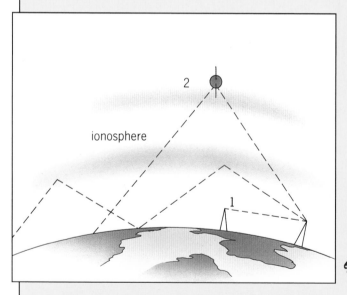

ionosphere

2

1

Telephone calls often travel by radio. They might be sent from one transmitter directly to a receiver (1). Radio signals can be sent to receivers beyond the horizon by bouncing them off the ionosphere, a layer of charged particles in the atmosphere. But telephone calls are usually relayed by satellites orbiting the Earth (2). They are so far away that there is a delay of several seconds before the answer to a question comes back during a call relayed by satellite.

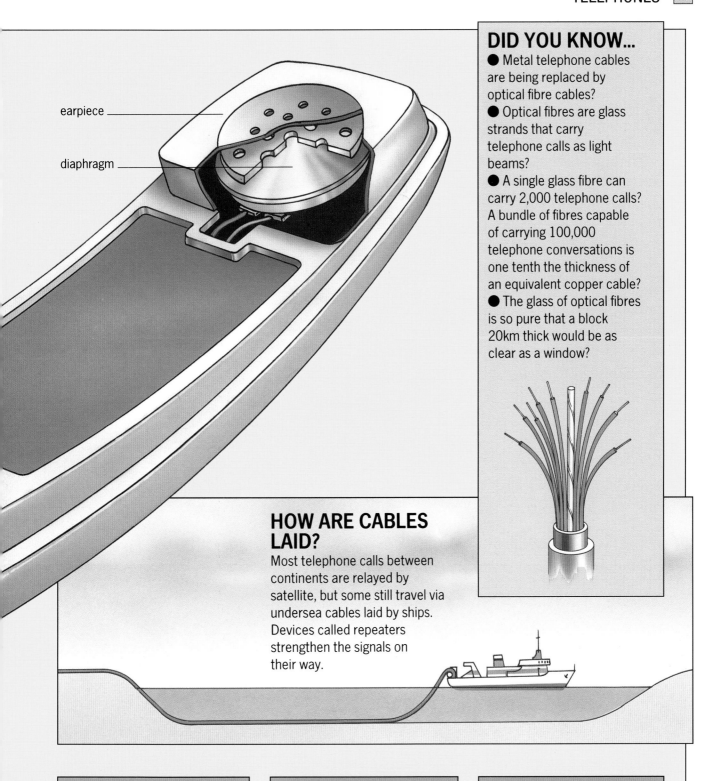

earpiece

diaphragm

DID YOU KNOW...
● Metal telephone cables are being replaced by optical fibre cables?
● Optical fibres are glass strands that carry telephone calls as light beams?
● A single glass fibre can carry 2,000 telephone calls? A bundle of fibres capable of carrying 100,000 telephone conversations is one tenth the thickness of an equivalent copper cable?
● The glass of optical fibres is so pure that a block 20km thick would be as clear as a window?

HOW ARE CABLES LAID?
Most telephone calls between continents are relayed by satellite, but some still travel via undersea cables laid by ships. Devices called repeaters strengthen the signals on their way.

HOW OLD IS IT?
The telephone was invented more than 100 years ago, in 1876, by the Scots-born American scientist, Alexander Graham Bell.

HOW MANY ARE THERE?
There are about 450 million telephones in the world. The United States has more telephones and makes more calls than any other country.

CAN I CALL FROM A CAR?
Yes – a mobile telephone has a built-in radio transmitter and receiver to link it to the rest of the international telephone network.

How does a stylus play music on a disc?

A gramophone disc, or record, is played by placing it on a turntable driven by an electric motor. A needle-like stylus rests in a groove in the record. There is just one groove, which spirals from the edge into the centre of the record. As the record spins, the stylus vibrates and a crystal or a coil of wire near a magnet change the vibrations into an electrical signal. This is strengthened by an amplifier and turned into sound by a loudspeaker.

A pick-up turns vibrations into electricity.

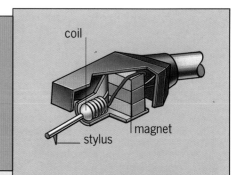

coil

stylus

magnet

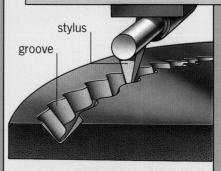

stylus

groove

record on turntable

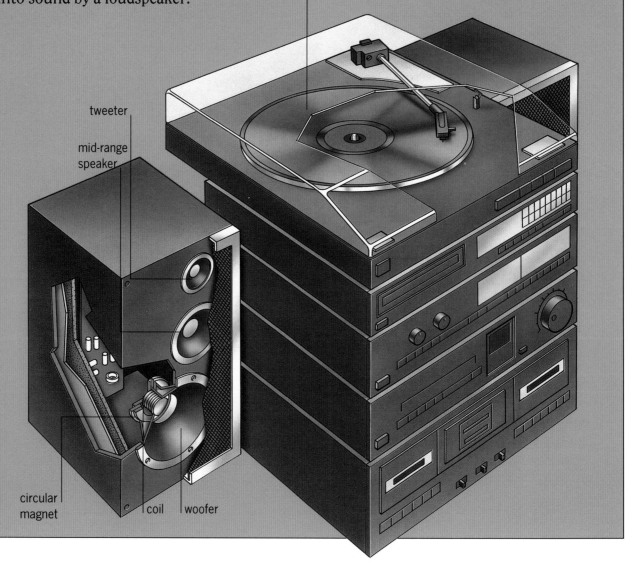

tweeter

mid-range speaker

circular magnet

coil

woofer

How do CDs work?

In the 1980s, a new way of playing music became popular. The compact disc (CD) has a shiny metal coating covered by clear plastic. Inside a CD player, a laser beam is focussed onto a spot a thousandth of a millimetre across on the disc which is spinning at up to 500rpm. The laser follows a track of pits etched (eaten) into the surface. The pits are less than a 2,000th of a millimetre long. As the disc spins, the spot is reflected by the metal but not by the pits. The reflection of the spot flickers. The flickering is picked up by a detector and changed into an electrical signal which is amplified and routed to a loudspeaker.

DID YOU KNOW...
● The laser light that shines on a CD is different from any other type of light?
● Sunlight is made from light waves of different lengths (colours) all jumbled together randomly?
● A laser beam is an intense shaft of light in which all the waves are the same length and line up with each other?
● Most lasers are gas-filled glass tubes tens of centimetres long, too big for use in a CD player, so a thumb-nail sized "solid state" laser on a chip was designed for use in CD players?

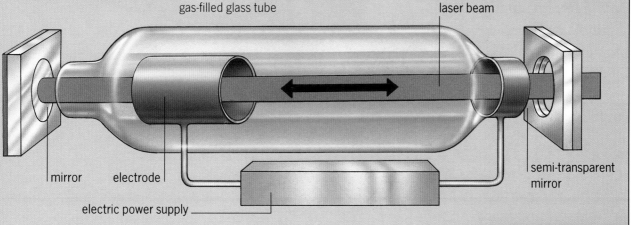

gas-filled glass tube

laser beam

mirror   electrode

electric power supply

semi-transparent mirror

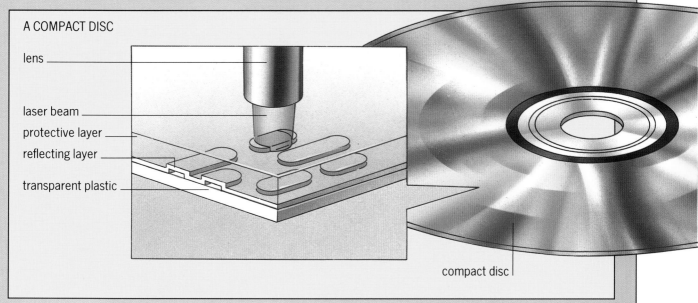

A COMPACT DISC

lens

laser beam

protective layer

reflecting layer

transparent plastic

compact disc

How does my radio set work?

The air is full of invisible radio waves spreading out from radio stations. When they fall on the aerial in your radio set, or receiver, they produce minute electric currents. Circuits inside the radio select, or "tune in", the signals you want from the many others received. Other circuits amplify the electric currents from the aerial and a loudspeaker turns them into sound waves.

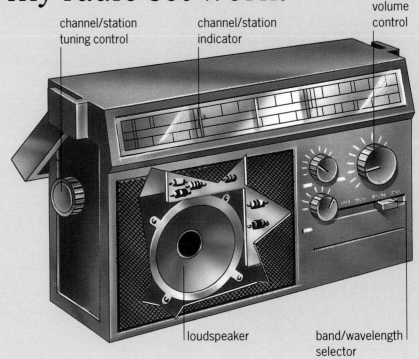

channel/station tuning control

channel/station indicator

volume control

loudspeaker

band/wavelength selector

How do radio signals travel?

Sound picked up by microphones in a radio studio is mixed with a high frequency signal, the carrier wave. This process, modulation, enables the signals to spread out from a transmitter as radio waves. Your radio picks them up, demodulates them (takes out the carrier wave) and turns them into sound again.

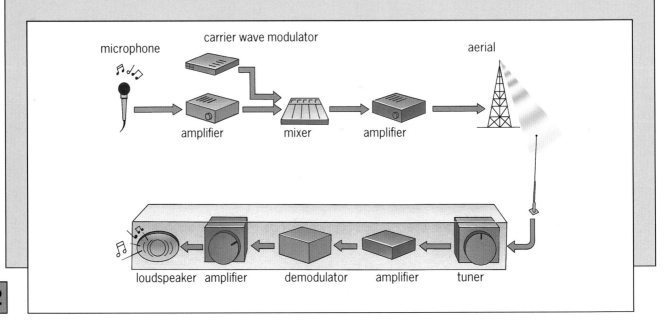

microphone

carrier wave modulator

aerial

amplifier

mixer

amplifier

loudspeaker   amplifier   demodulator   amplifier   tuner

How does my TV make colour pictures?

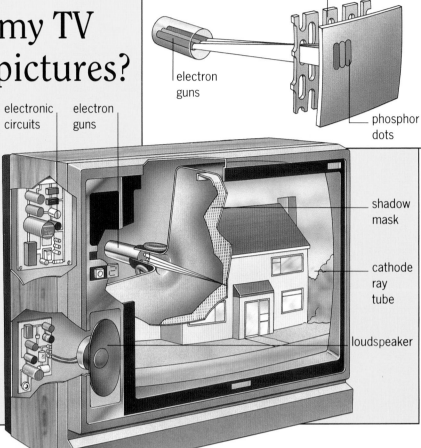

shadow mask

electron guns

phosphor dots

The back of a TV screen is coated with phosphors, materials that glow when hit by electrons (tiny particles). Three beams of electrons trace out lines across the screen, passing through holes in the shadow mask so that each lights up a different set of phosphor dots – one red, one green and one blue. The dots and lines merge to form the picture.

electronic circuits

electron guns

shadow mask

cathode ray tube

loudspeaker

Why are TV aerials so shaped?

Most TV aerials are shaped like metal trees and point at the nearest transmitter on the ground. Dish-shaped aerials point at a satellite in space. TV programmes are beamed up to the satellite which re-transmits them down to Earth. Many ground transmitters are needed to reach all parts of a country, but a whole country can be covered by one satellite transmitter.

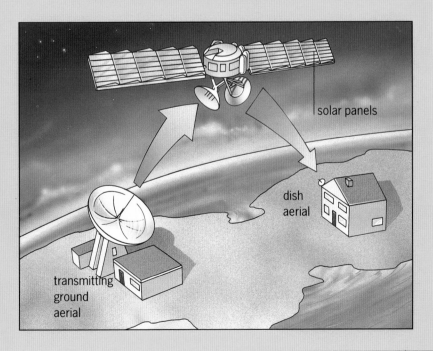

solar panels

dish aerial

transmitting ground aerial

How is a tape recording made?

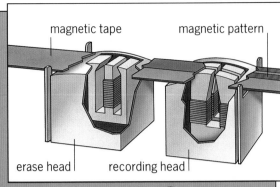

magnetic tape   magnetic pattern

erase head   recording head

Sound is first converted into electric currents which pass through a coil of wire wrapped around a piece of iron, the recording head. The iron is magnetised and the changing current changes the strength of the magnet. As the tape passes over a narrow gap in the head, magnetic particles in the tape move to line up with its changing magnetic field. In this way, a magnetic copy of the original sounds is created on the tape. A second electromagnet, the erase head, wipes the tape clean before each new recording is made. The tape can be used many times.

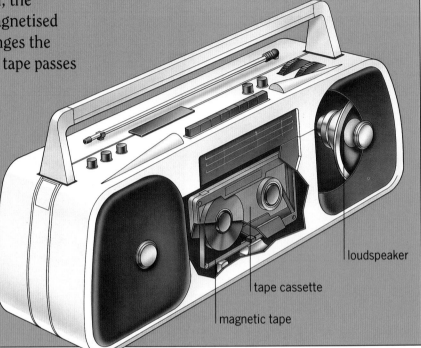

loudspeaker

tape cassette

magnetic tape

What do microphones do?

There are different types of microphone, but they all do the same job. They change sound into an electric signal. Inside the moving coil microphone shown here, a diaphragm vibrates when sound hits it. A coil of wire fixed to the diaphragm, and also inside a magnet, vibrates too. The wire vibrating in the magnetic field produces an electric current in the wire which varies in step with the sound.

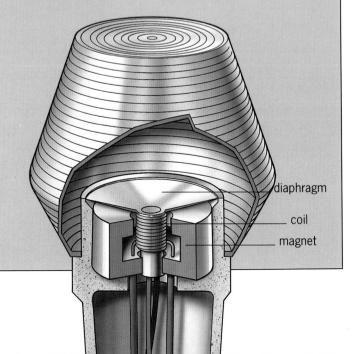

diaphragm

coil

magnet

How does a video recorder work?

When you push a cassette into a video recorder to record a TV programme, a loop of tape is pulled out of the cassette and wrapped around a spinning drum containing the video recording heads.

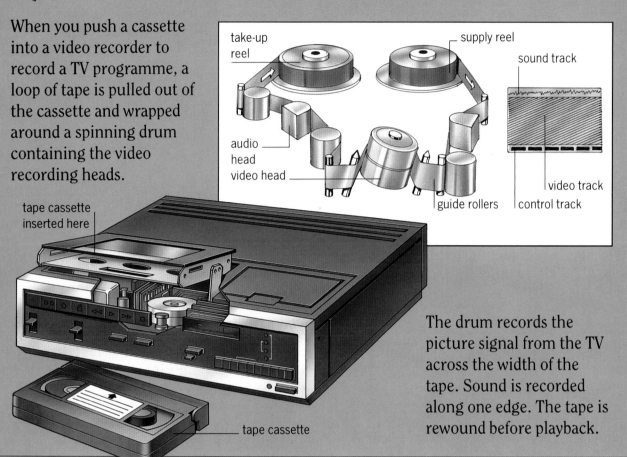

take-up reel

supply reel

sound track

audio head

video head

guide rollers

control track

video track

tape cassette inserted here

tape cassette

The drum records the picture signal from the TV across the width of the tape. Sound is recorded along one edge. The tape is rewound before playback.

Can a video disc store pictures?

Yes. A video disc is like a CD except that it holds pictures as well as sound. A laser beam is reflected by the spinning disc's metal coating but not by pits in the metal. The flickering reflection is changed into an electric signal and a TV set turns it into pictures and sound.

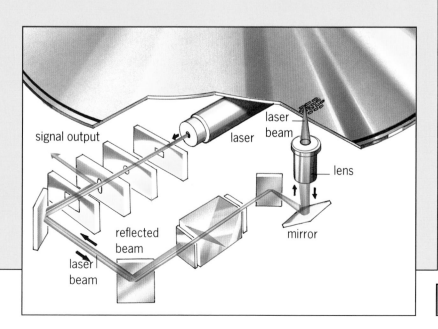

signal output

laser

laser beam

lens

reflected beam

mirror

laser beam

45

What happens when I take a picture?

A camera is a light-tight box with a lens at the front and light-sensitive film inside. A diaphragm in the lens opens and closes to control the amount of light entering the camera. When you press a button (the shutter release) to take a picture, the shutter opens and light is focussed on the film.

DID YOU KNOW...
● The first photographs, produced in the early 1800s, were made on light-sensitive metal or glass plates?
● Colour film (invented in the 1930s) is three films in one – one layer responds to blue light, one to red and one to green – which together form a full colour picture?
● Some cameras are focussed automatically by using an infra-red beam to measure how far away the subject is?

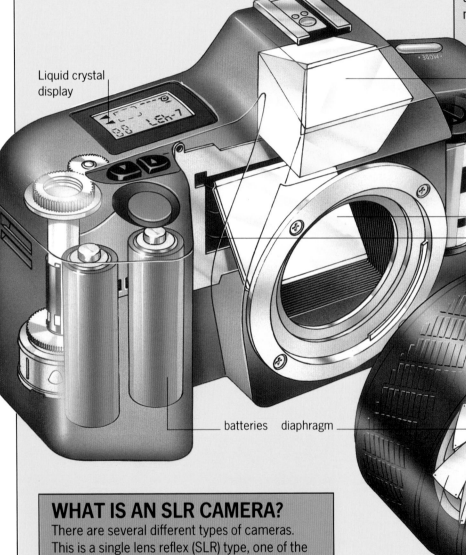

Liquid crystal display

viewfinder

film container

mirror

film

batteries   diaphragm

lens

WHAT IS AN SLR CAMERA?
There are several different types of cameras. This is a single lens reflex (SLR) type, one of the most popular. This one has a small liquid crystal display (LCD) that shows its settings and an electric motor to wind the film on after each photograph is taken.

HOW MANY LENSES?

Most cameras have two lenses. The photographer points the camera by looking through one and the other focusses light onto the film. The single lens reflex (SLR) camera improves on this by showing the photographer exactly the same image that the film will record. Light entering the single lens is reflected up to the viewfinder by a mirror and a specially shaped piece of glass. When the shutter release button is pressed, the mirror swings up for a moment to let the light pass through onto the film.

FAST PHOTOS

A modern SLR camera can open its shutter for as little as a thousandth of a second. Taking a photograph in such a short time freezes all the movement in the image and makes a sharp picture.

HOW ARE PHOTOS MADE?

When you take a photograph, light falling on the film changes a few molecules of silver salts in the film into pure silver. The effect is so slight that the image is invisible. The first stage in producing a photograph is to treat the film with chemicals to multiply this effect millions of times over until the "latent" (invisible) image becomes visible. The second stage involves projecting light through the developed film onto light sensitive paper and then developing this chemically to make each photograph.

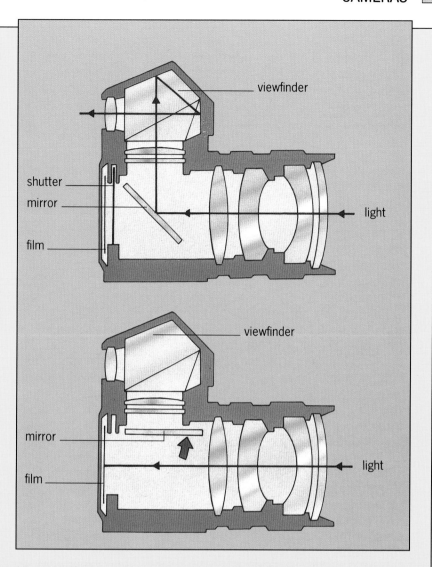

viewfinder

shutter

mirror

film

light

viewfinder

mirror

film

light

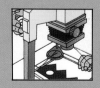

The film is placed inside a light-tight tank and chemicals

are poured in to develop the pictures on it.

The developed film is projected onto photographic paper,

which is itself developed to make a print.

INDEX

aerial 42, 43
air conditioning 19
alternative energy 8
amp (ampere) 4
atoms 6, 7

bar code 15
battery 10
Bell, Alexander Graham 39
Benz, Karl 12
black-out 5
blast furnace 22
blood filter 20
body scanner 21
brown-out 5
brush, motor 10

cables, electricity 5
cameras 46, 47
camshaft 12
Carlson, Chester 17
chain reaction 7
clocks 34
coal 6, 28
coal mine 28
coil 10, 11
combustion chamber 13
commutator 10, 11
compact disc, CD 41, 45
compressor turbine 13
computer 14, 15
Concorde 13
connecting rod 12
crankshaft 12

dams 9
dialysis 20
discs 40
drive wheel 34

electric
    current 4, 5, 42
    iron 33
    motors 10, 11
    train 11
electricity 4, 5, 6, 8, 9, 10, 11
electronic calculator 35
energy
    alternative 8
    nuclear 6
engine
    jet 13

petrol 12
escalator 19
escapement, clock 34

facsimile, fax 17
fan belt 12
Faraday, Michael 11
flat plate collector 9
floppy disc 14
fuel rods 6

gas turbine 13
gears 12
generator 4, 6, 9, 12
gravure 31

household appliances 32
hydrocarbon 27
hydroelectricity 9
hydrogen 7

iron 22

keys 36
kidney machine 20

laser 15, 41
letterpress 31
lift 18
liquid crystal display, LCD 35
lithography 31
lock
    cylinder 36
    lever-tumbler 37

magnet 10, 11
magnetic force 4
magnetism 11
memory chip 14
metal 22
microphone 44
microprocessor 14
mining 24
modulation 42
music 40

national grid 5
neutrons 7
nuclear fission 7
nuclear fusion 7
nuclear power 8
nucleus 6

oil 12, 24, 25, 26
    filter 12
    production 25
    refining 27

paper 30
papermaking 30
petrochemicals 26
petrol 12
photocopier, photocopy 16, 17
photodetector 15
photograph 46
piston 12
plastics 26, 27
polymer 27
polythene 27
power cut 5
power stations 4, 5, 6, 7
printing 30
printing press 31
program, computer 14
pulp, wood 30

radio 42
reactor 6, 7
record 40
recording equipment 44
refrigerator, fridge 32
reservoir 9
rotor 10, 11

skyscraper 18, 19
sound 42
spark plug 12
stator 10, 11
steam 4, 5
steel 22
steelmaking 23
sump 12

tape recording 44
telephone 38, 39
    exchange 38
television, TV 43
TGV 11
timekeepers 34
timing belt 12
tomography 21
transformer 5
turbines 4, 5, 6, 9
turbofan 13
turbojet 13

ultrasound 21
uranium 6, 7

vacuum cleaner 32
valve 12
video recorder 45
vision 42
volt 4

washing machine 33
watches 34
water 29
water treatment 29
waterwheel 8
windmill 8

x-ray 21
xerography 16, 17